FAST TRACK
to Reading Success
Smarty, Dummy, and the Bad

FAST TRACK

WALKER GUE

outskirts
press

TABLE OF CONTENTS

Chapter 1: Awaken the genius inside your children's minds: 1

Chapter 2: Mama the Sorcerer 5

Chapter 3: Brush Your Teeth 9

Chapter 4: Ticket 10

Chapter 5: 40 Acres of Land 13

Chapter 6: Forty Acres of Land 16

Chapter 7: Buy a Car 18

Chapter 8: Goal Setting 19

Chapter 9: The Engagement 20

Chapter 10: The Meeting 22

Chapter 11: The Second Meeting: 23

Chapter 12: Our Minds 24

Chapter 13: The Housecleaner and Her Attitude: 26

Chapter 14: Attitude 28

Chapter 15: The Mother Goat ok 30

Chapter 16: The Loser Left His Wife 32

Chapter 17: Courtesy 33

Chapter 18: The Procrastinator 35

Chapter 1
AWAKEN THE GENIUS INSIDE YOUR CHILDREN'S MINDS:

If your students are four years old, they are most likely already good readers. If not, here is the **solution**. Note that individual results may vary due to the fact each child is different. Your mind is the same as lovely flowers; if you fertilize it the right way, beautiful things will grow. It is the greatest gift our creator has given us. Why does this **technique work**? I could have written a book on the **why**; however, I am so happy to finally get to present the solution. Each time I said, "Tomorrow I will work on the solution," then I would find some excuse not to generate the knowledge.

Now let us commence on the right way to activate your children into fast readers. Tell your friends about this book. I am strongly confident you will see results right away. The school cannot do it alone. As parents you need to take the initiative to help your children. Teachers, inform parents of this book.

First, you need to arrange each word in a vertical order. Second, with a pencil point at the first word and say, "This word is _____" and say the word. Have your child repeat the word, then turn the page to the paragraph and tell your student to find the word and underline it. Continue the process until you finish the whole page. Repeat this process for a few days, then engage your students in reading by pointing at each word as you say it, and have your child repeat the word in the paragraph after you.

Example, ask your student to find the word mama, the, sorcerer, lives, in, a, etc.

Finally, have your child read the whole page alone.

This technique is the best.

Mama	has	for	who	many	boys	lives	her	and
The	many	her	has	toys	with	it	broomstick	said
Sorcerer	cats	cat	many	and	so	is	While	Hello
lives	One	and	toys	she	many	getting	she	there
In	Monday	she	she	has	toys	late	was	do
a	she	hears	knows	an	lives	so	way	you
faraway	decides	every	that	idea	No	she	up	know
mountain	to	one	her	she	one	decides	in	where
with	go	talking	cat	decides	seems	to	the	Hayden
many	the	about	has	to	to	go	sky	lives
trees	market	a	always	ask	know	home	she	The
There	to	boy	wanted	people	where	She	met	bird
she	buy	name	to	where	this	jumps	a	replies
has	food	Hayden	have	this	boy	on	bird	Yes
I	arrive	mama	make	happy	and	and		
Know	birdy	is	mama	she	said	share		
Are	shows	looking	happy	decides	who	his		
You	Hayden's	at	the	to	is it	toys		
Talking	school	everything	most	land	Me	Hayden's		
about	and	in	is	down	mama	mother		
the	his	Hayden's	that	in	the	says		
boy	house	back	Hayden	front	sorcerer	come		
with	She	yard	has cars	of	I	on		
lot	is	She	with	Hayden	heard	in		
of	so	notices	so	house	that	have		
toys	happy	Hayden	many	She	Hayden	a seat		
Mama	and	has	different	walks	has	she		
Replies	says	a	colors	up	so	walks		
Yes	Thanks	truck	red	in	many	upstairs		
The	birdy	scooter	blue	front	toys	calls		
Birdy	and	bicycles	purple	of	I	Hayden		
Says	the	race	green	Hayden's	would	and says		

To follow	birdy	car	black	door	like	Mama	
him	replies	remote	yellow	and	to	the	
and	no	car	white	knocks	play	sorcerer	
he	problem	and	orange	on	with	is	
will	way	a	pink	his	him	downstairs	
show	up	remote	gray	door	and		
her	in	control	and	Hayden's	she		
When	the	airplane	brown	mother	would		
they	sky	What	She	is	so	walks to the door	like

The **key** is to say, "Find the word in the paragraph and underline it as if the word is playing hide and seek." This will maximize, motivate, and activate an academic interest in reading. This is how children start reading right away. Some would have paid a million dollars to find the right way. <u>Here it is</u>.

to	she	brown	Hayden	and	toys
play	says	rice	there	cars	for
with	My	baked	mama	Mama	her
you	boy	chicken	went	says	cat
and	look	and	up	it is	
share	at	cereal	and	getting	
your	you	in	down	late	
toys	have	the	the	it is	
yes	getting	morning	slide	time	
mother	taller	good	Next	to	go
I	and	mama	mama	home	
Will	bigger	says	goes	and	
come	what is	now	on	feed	
down	your	let	the	my	
Soon	mother	us	swing	cat	
to	have	go	then	Before	
play	been	outside	rides	she	
with	feeding	in	the	get	

mama	you	the	bicycles	on		
As	All	backyard	and	her		
Hayden	type	and	plays	broomstick		
comes	of	play	with	she		
down	food	Mama	the	asks		
to	mostly	goes	remote	Hayden		
greet	vegetable	outside	control	for		
mama	and	fruit	with	airplane	some	toys
for	for	before				
her	mama	you				
cat	Goodbye	come				
sure	Hayden	Mama				
mama	next	jumps				
which	time	on				
one	may	I her				
of	come	broomstick				
my	with	and				
toys	my	flies				
would	cat	up				
you	to	in				
like	play	the				
Hayden	with	sky				
Asks	you	Bye	mama			
She	sure					
Says	mama					
give	call					
me	me					
the red	on					
car	the					
the purple car						
and the green car						

Chapter 2
MAMA THE SORCERER

Find the words in the paragraph and underline them.

Mama the sorcerer lives in a faraway mountain with many trees. There she has many cats. One Monday, she decides to go to the market to buy food for her cat, and she hears everyone talking about a boy named Hayden who has many toys. She knows that her cat has always wanted to have many toys, and she has an idea. She decides to ask people where this boy with many toys lives. No one seems to know where this boy lives. It is getting late so she decides to go home. She jumps on her broomstick. While she is way up in the sky, she meets a bird and says, "Hello there, do you know where Hayden lives?"

The bird replies, "Yes, I know. Are you talking about the boy with a lot of toys?"

Mama replies, "Yes."

The bird says to follow him and he will show her. When they arrive, the bird shows Mama Hayden's school and his house. She is so happy, and says, "Thanks, birdy," and the bird replies, "No problem."

Way up in the sky, Mama is looking at everything in Hayden's backyard. She notices Hayden has a truck, scooter, bicycles, racecar, a remote-control car, and a remote-control airplane. What makes Mama the most happy is that Hayden has cars with so many different colors: red, blue, purple, green, black, yellow, white, orange, pink, gray, and brown. She is so happy she decides to land in front of Hayden's house.

She walks up and knocks on his door. Hayden's mother walks to the door and says, "Who is it?"

"Me, Mama the sorcerer! I heard that Hayden has many toys. I would like to play with him and share his toys."

Hayden's mother says, "Come on in, have a seat." She walks upstairs, calls Hayden, and says, "Mama the sorcerer is downstairs and she would like to play with you and share your toys."

"Yes, Mother, I will come down soon to play with Mama."

When Hayden comes down to greet Mama, she says, "My boy, look at you; you have gotten taller and bigger. What has your mother been feeding you?"

"All types of food; mostly vegetables and fruit, brown rice, baked chicken, and cereal in the morning."

"Good," Mama says, "now let's go outside in the backyard and play."

Mama goes outside with Hayden; there she goes up and down the slide. Next Mama goes on the swing, then rides the bicycles and plays with the remote-control airplane and cars. Mama says it is getting late; it is time to go home and feed her cat. Before she gets on her broomstick, she asks Hayden for some toys for her cat.

"Sure, Mama, which one of my toys would you like?" Hayden asks.

She says, "Give me the red car, the purple car, and the green car please." Hayden puts the cars in a box for Mama.

"Goodbye, Hayden. Next time may I come with my cat to play with you?"

"Sure, Mama, call me on the phone before you come."

Mama jumps on her broomstick and flies up in the sky. Bye, Mama.

Brush
Your
Teeth
A
Woman
named
Josephine
has
two
sons
whom
she
loves
very
much
Dummy
Dummy
he
goes
to
bed
at
night
he
does
definitely
have
a
cavity
should
I
do

not
brush
his
teeth
and
refuses
to
take
a
shower
His
younger
brother
Smarty
says
to
the
it
is
not
a
good
habit
to
go
you
go
to
bed
thank
you
doctor

bed
without
brushing
your
teeth
Dummy
replies
no
brother
it
feels
good
to
sleep
with
all
will
food
in
my
mouth
Well
our
mother
and

father
said
we
should
brush
our
teeth
so
we
don't
develop
cavities
I
don't
think
I
Smarty
cavities
notices
only
bad
boy
get
cavities
he
continues

his
bad
habit
of
not
brushing
his
teeth
at
night
rarely
in
the
morning
one
night
hurting
notices
that
Dummy
is
crying
in
bed
and

cannot
sleep
Dummy
what
is
the
matter
and
why
are
you
not
sleeping
Brother
tooth
is
cavity
me
what
can
it
be
brother
let
me

see
inside
your
mouth
Smarty
sees
a
cavity
in
one
of
Dummy's
teeth
you
have
a
they
Smarty
says
what
should
I
do
brother
well

tell
dad
so
that
he
can
bring
you
to
the
dental
office
at
the
dental
office
before
told
Dummy
you

doctor   from

well   now

you   on

should   I

brush   will

your   brush

teeth   my   teeth

3   before

Times   I

a   go

day

especially   to

after   bed

you

finish

eating

and

at

night

before

Chapter 3
BRUSH YOUR TEETH

A woman named Josephine has two sons whom she loves very much. Dummy, before he goes to bed at night, does not brush his teeth and refuses to take a shower. His younger brother Smarty says to Dummy, "It is not a good habit to go to bed without brushing your teeth."

Dummy replies, "No, brother, it feels good to sleep with the smell and the taste of the food in my mouth."

"Well, our mother and father said we should brush our teeth so that we don't develop cavities. Dad said that if you have a cavity, the other teeth in your mouth can develop cavities also."

Dummy says, "I don't think I will ever have cavities. Only bad boys have cavities." He continues his bad habit of not brushing his teeth at night and rarely brushing them in the morning.

One night Smarty notices that Dummy is crying in bed and cannot sleep. "Dummy, what is the matter, why are you not sleeping?"

"Brother, my tooth is hurting me; what can it be, brother?"

"Let me see inside your mouth." Smarty sees a cavity in one of Dummy's teeth. "You have a cavity," Smarty says.

"What should I do, brother?"

"Well, tell Dad so that he can bring you to the dental office."

At the dental office, they tell Dummy, "You definitely have a cavity."

"What should I do, Doctor?"

"Well, you should brush your teeth three times a day, especially after you finish eating and at night before you go to bed."

"Thank you, Doctor. From now on I will brush my teeth before I go to bed," Dummy says.

Chapter 4
TICKET

Two brothers, Smarty and Dummy, have their driver's licenses. One Monday morning, the older brother, Dummy, decides to drive his car to school. His younger brother, Smarty, notices that Dummy is driving his car too fast and does not stop at the stop sign. Smarty says to his older brother, "You are driving too fast. That is dangerous and you must stop at the stop sign."

Dummy replies, "Oh no, it is fun to drive fast and not stop at a stop sign. That way you can get wherever you are going quicker."

Smarty says, "If you don't slow down, you can get a ticket from the police, and if you are stopped by the police, you should say that you are sorry and that you will be more careful."

It is not long after that the two brothers go to a party and Dummy starts drinking. Smarty says to Dummy, "You should not drink, because you will drive us home later."

The older brother replies, "Oh no, a drink or two will not hurt."

When it is time to go home, Dummy refuses to let his younger brother drive home. While driving Dummy is stopped by a police officer because he did not stop at a stop sign. When the officer approaches him, Dummy is disrespectful, so he gets a ticket.

On Tuesday morning, Smarty decides to go to school with his own car, refusing to ride with Dummy. "Well, brother, since I have been the one doing most of the driving to get to school, from now on I would rather that you drive," Dummy says.

"Sure," Smarty replies. "It is my pleasure; I would love to drive you."

This time Smarty is making a right turn at the corner and forgets to turn his signal on, and a police officer notices. He stops Smarty, asks him for his driver's license, and tells him he did not turn his right turn signal on.

Smarty replies, "I am sorry, sir, I totally forgot. I will be more careful."

The police officer asks Smarty, "Where are you going?"

Nicely, Smarty replies, "I am on my way to school, sir."

The officer says, "You are excused. Try to be more careful."

"Yes, sir," Smarty replies.

Smarty is not given a ticket.

Find each word in the paragraph and underline the word.

Two	his	his	fun	Smarty	drive	the	stop	excused
brothers	younger	older	to	says	Dummy	corner	Smarty	try
have	brother	brother	drive	if	says	and	asks	to
their	smarty	you	fast	you	sure	forgets	Smarty	be
driving	notices	are	and	don't	his	to	Where	more
licenses	that	driving	not	slow	brother	turn	are	careful
are	Dummy	too	stop	down	Smarty	on	you	yes
Smarty	is	fast	at	you	replies	his	going	sir
And	driving	that	the	can	It	is	signal	nicely
Dummy	his	is	stop sign	get	my	to	Smarty	replies
One	car	dangerous	a	pleasure	show	replies	Smarty	
Monday	too	and	That	ticket	I	that	I	is
Morning	fast	you	way	from	would	he	am	not
the	and	must	you	the	love	is	on	given
older	does	stop	can	police	to	making	my	a
brother	not	at	get	and	drive	a	way	ticket
Dummy	stop	the	wherever	if	you	right	to	
decides	at	stop	you	you	this time	turn	school	
to	the	sign	are	are	Smarty	and	Sir	
drives	stop	Dummy	going	stop	is	a police	the	
his	sign	replies	quicker	by	making	officer	police	
car	Smarty	Oh	police	a right	notices	officer		
to	says	no	you	turn	that	you		
school	to	it	is	say	at	he	are	
that	Dummy	go	the	to				
you	you	home	officer	take				
are	should	Dummy	approaches	a				
sorry	not	refuses	him	ride				
and	drink	to let	Dummy	with				
that	because	his	is	Dummy				
you	you	younger	disrespectful					

more	will	brother	to	Well
careful	drive	drive	the	brother
it	us	home	officer	since
is	home	While	so	have
not	later	driving	he	the
long	the older	Dummy	get	one
after	brother	is stopped	a ticket	doing
that	replies	by	On	most
the	oh	the	Tuesday	of
two	no	police	morning	driving
brothers	a	officer	Smarty	to
goes	drink	because	Smarty	get
to	or	he	decides	to
a party	two	did	to go	school
and	will	not	to	for
Dummy	not	stop	school	now on
Starts	hurt	at	with his	I
drinking	When	the	own	will
Smarty	it is	stop	car	rather
Says	time	sign	refuses	that
To	to	when	you	

Chapter 5
40 ACRES OF LAND

Smarty
And
Dummy
were
given
40
acre
of
land
by
their
grand
mother
who
was
98
Years
Old
This
Land
Had
Been

family
for
a
long
time
had
nothing
done
to
it
for
because
it
had
so
many
rocks
and
a
very
high
mountain

in
the
middle
of
it
No
one
wanted
this
land
anything
on
it
or
cultivated it
because
it
would
require
hard
work
One

noticed
too
much
grass
growing
on
the
land
so
she
decided
to
call
Smarty
and
Dummy
to do
something
with
Dummy
said
land

many
rocks
and
trees
sold
his
portion
to
his
to
brother
Smarty
for
100
dollars
Dummy
said
that
it
to
his
younger

and
told
him
he
was
going
to
the
city
discouraged
look
for
a
high
paying
job
and

goodbye
work
is
too

good
luck
with
the
hard
work
Smarty
was
not

farm

In	right	day	had	brother	hard.
their	in	grandma	too	Smarty	

Smarty	vegetables	his	good	noticed	put	the
Decided	he	second	luck	that	it	more
To	liked	goal	with	the	in	he
Start	such	was	hard	color	a	dug
Working	as	to	work	of	container	the
On	spinach	start	smarty	the	and	more
His	carrots	cutting	was	dirt	put	yellow
Land	potatoes	a	not	changed	it	dirt
By	sweet	in	discouraged	to	under	came
Cleaning	yams	half	and	dark	wood	he
All	and	so	continued	brown	fire	walked
The	corn	he	with	to	the	home
Wild	one	can	his	yellow	dirt	and
Grass	day	create	plan	smarty	started	told
And	smarty	a	as	realized	to	his
Trees	wrote	roadway	smarty	what	melt	grandpa
Grandpa	a	his	started	it	to	what
Was	letter	older	cutting	was	solid	he
Really	to	brother	the	he	to	had
Proud	his	sent	mountain	took	liquid	found
Of	older	a	and	the	gold	it
Him	brother	letter	digging	yellow	he	turned
Smarty	dummy	and	dirt	heavy	continued	out
Started	telling	told	out	dirt	digging	big
Planting	him	him	he	and	up	the
Big	behind	was	rocks	Dummy	had	
High	it	a huge	were	went	given	

Mountain Had So Much Gold It Could Fill Up A Whole house He woke Up In the morning and take a bath behind the mountain Because

was a river as he was swimming he looked down and noticed shiny rock the river he broke this rock in half and inside the rock there

diamond he continue to look for in same type of rock a again this rock had a huge piece of diamond it turn out all the

diamond he ran home his grandma the was very happy grandma and Smarty that this river which was attached to the land was also his Meanwhile

in the city looking for a she paying job Smarty sent told brother a letter telling him what he had found that the land that grandma

them which look dirty hard work higher out to be a his of diamond and gold

turn

land

Chapter 6
FORTY ACRES OF LAND

Smarty and Dummy were given forty acres of land by their grandmother, who was ninety-eight years old. This land had been in their family for a long time. This land had nothing done to it because it had so many rocks and a very high mountain right in the middle of it. No one wanted this land, built anything on it, or cultivated it because it would require hard work. One day, Grandma noticed too much grass growing on the land, so she decided to call Smarty and Dummy to do something with it. Dummy said the land had too many rocks and trees, and that the land would require too much hard work, so he sold his portion to his brother Smarty for a hundred dollars. Dummy said goodbye to his younger brother Smarty and told him he was going to the city to look for a high-paying job and that farm work was too hard.

Smarty decided to start working on his land, cleaning all the wild grass and cutting down the trees. Grandma was very proud of him. Smarty started planting all the vegetables Grandma liked, such as spinach, carrots, potatoes, sweet yams, and corn. One day Smarty wrote a letter to his older brother Dummy, telling him his second goal was to start cutting the mountain in half so that he could create a roadway. His older brother sent him a letter and told him good luck with that hard work. Smarty was not discouraged and continued with his plan. As Smarty started cutting the mountain and digging dirt out, he noticed that the color of the dirt started changing from a dark brown to yellow. Smarty realized what it was. He took the heavy yellow dirt, put it in a large container, and put wood fire under the container. The dirt started melting from solid to liquid gold. He continued digging up the mountain. The more he dug the more yellow dirt started showing up. He walked home and told his grandma what he had found; it turned out that the big, high mountain had so much gold that it was enough to fill his whole house. He woke up in the morning to take a bath because behind the mountain there was a river. As he started swimming in the river, he looked down and noticed a shiny rock. He broke this rock in half, and inside the rock, there was a huge diamond. He continued to look for the same type of rock, and again this rock had a huge piece of a diamond. It turned out that, in this river, all the dirty rocks were diamond. He ran home and told his grandma. She was very happy and told Smarty that this river, which was attached to the land, was also his. Meanwhile Dummy went to the city looking for a higher paying job.

Smarty sent his older brother Dummy a letter telling him what he had found, that the land Grandma had given them, which looked like dirty, hard work, turned out to be a land of diamonds and gold.

Smarty told Dummy, "Diamonds and gold may look dirty, but it takes a person with wisdom to figure out what diamonds and gold really are."

Chapter 7
BUY A CAR

Smarty and Dummy receive forty dollars each from their grandma to purchase a car. The younger brother, Smarty, tells his brother, "When you are ready to purchase your car, let me know so that I can go with you to make sure you get a good car."

Dummy says, "No, I will go by myself. I do not need your opinion. Besides, I am older than you. I can make my own choices."

"Never mind," Smarty answers.

On a Wednesday, Dummy wakes up early in the morning and leaves the house by himself to purchase his own car. He decides to purchase an old car for four dollars. For the first twelve months, the car drives great, no problems; then the car's transmission breaks, and he spends ten dollars to fix it. Then the car engine breaks, and he spends ten dollars to fix it. Then the car has electrical problems, and he spends ten dollars to fix it. After that the power steering breaks, and he spends six dollars to fix it. Lastly he realizes the car needs new brakes and the car's paint is fading away.

"Oh no, why does this car keep breaking down?" he asks his younger brother Smarty.

Smarty replies, "If you had taken the time to listen to me, you would have done the same thing that I did. I bought myself a new car for twenty-five dollars. I wake up in the morning knowing that I don't have to worry that the car will break down, and I also have insurance to protect the car just in case something breaks. The car manufacturer will fix it, and if they cannot fix it, they will give me another new car."

Chapter 8
GOAL SETTING

Smarty and Dummy, two students, have their own habits. When Smarty is in class and the teacher is talking, giving information on a particular subject, this is the time Dummy finds it convenient to carry out his conversation. Everyone in class is annoyed with his behavior, preventing the other student from concentrating and focusing. The teacher doesn't like it either, often having to tell him, "When you are in class, this is not the time to have a conversation." Most students in class think he has bad manners.

When school ends at 2:30 p.m., Dummy is at home by 2:45. He plays his games until 6:00 and at 6:30 he picks up his bicycle, goes out for a ride, and comes home at 8:45. At 9:00 p.m. he has his dinner and takes a shower by 10:00. He watches TV until 10:30 p.m., and after that he remembers he has homework to do. Sometimes he forgets to do his homework.

Smarty, on the other hand, once he comes from school tackles his homework right away. He does not watch TV or play games. He puts in eighteen hours a day in his studying and he does not fool around at all. Smarty says his goal is to put in a hundred hours per week in his studies, and his second goal is to become an inventor.

Who do you think will achieve more in life, Smarty or Dummy?

_____

And why?

_____

Chapter 9
THE ENGAGEMENT

Smarty and Dummy notice two beautiful girls in their neighborhood. In their tradition you cannot talk to the girl; you have to ask the parent of the girl first and they will decide if they want you for their daughter. If the mother of the girl doesn't like you, you might as well forget it. You will not have a chance of marrying her daughter. The father of the girl has no say in this matter. This subject by culture concerns only the girls, which are the mother and her daughters.

Smarty and Dummy, on a Thursday morning, go to Josephine's house, asking her if it is okay to allow her daughters to marry them. Josephine replies, "Well, tell me about you. I'd like to know about your background, such as education, profession, hobby, especially the type of music you like." However, Josephine makes an error and forgets to ask the boys about their culture.

"Dummy, you first," Josephine says. "Tell me about yourself."

"Well, my name is Dummy Glue. I have lived in this neighborhood for a very long time. I am a college graduate. I majored in business. People call me Mr. Prince because I am a rich man. I have done well in business, I love to play golf. and I listen to different kinds of music. Right now I am ready to get married, and I would love to marry one of your daughters, especially the one you love the most."

Josephine says, "Very good, Dummy, I will allow you to marry my most beautiful daughter, the one I love the most."

"Which one?" Dummy asks.

"Well, the older one. She is my favorite. I love her the most."

"Very well," Dummy says. "I do not want to waste time. I will marry her next week."

"So be it," Josephine says.

Josephine is very pleased with Dummy's answers, not to mention Dummy is more handsome than Smarty.

"Now," Josephine says to Smarty, "tell me about yourself."

"Well, I am a simple guy. I love to read and write. I am not rich. As a hobby I love to create products, I love classical music, and I am a family-oriented person. I respect people's culture, custom, and values."

"Oh well," Josephine says, "I know which one is right for you. My second daughter, she's my least favorite. She's so calm and has no excitement in her life. She will be perfect for you."

Little does Josephine know what Dummy is about to do. After Dummy marries the most beautiful and favorite daughter, he builds her a house all the way in Alaska. The place is very cold and far away. Sometimes a whole year goes by where Josephine cannot communicate with or see her favorite daughter. Not to mention, Josephine's culture and values cannot be passed to her grandchildren, especially her ancestors' language. She sees her grandchildren every five years. This situation makes Josephine sad and unhappy. Not to mention Dummy does not treat Josephine's favorite daughter like a princess. Often he does not remember his wife's birthday or his wedding anniversary and almost never calls his mother-in-law to find out how she is doing or if she needs help with anything.

Smarty, on the other hand, thinks that it is important for his wife to live near her mother; he thinks it is a beautiful thing for his children to speak the language of their ancestors and to practice and understand their grandma's culture.

And Smarty always remembers his wife's birthday and their anniversary. He is not rich but he finds the time to purchase a present for his wife and call his mother-in-law once a month. All Thanksgiving dinners occur at Grandma's house. Smarty is not the most handsome; he is cute with curly hair. He is not rich or a prince. However, he treats Josephine's second daughter like a princess and lives happily with whatever they have.

Smarty plants a beautiful garden for his wife, buys her roses and flowers for her birthday.

Most importantly, he adores, cherishes, loves, and respects his wife.

Chapter 10
THE MEETING

When Smarty and Dummy were in college, Smarty figured out something that revolutionized the way we send a letter, reducing long lines at the post office or in the bank, making communication and how we deposit money in the bank way faster. So Smarty first told his mother, his sister, his whole family, and some teachers what his plan was, and everyone said that sounded impossible or "If this is true, this will be like a miracle."

Dummy said, "No way, brother, how could anybody send a letter or a note to someone and within seconds, the person you are sending the note or letter receives it? That sounds impossible to me, brother. How can you do that?"

"I would not do it. I will invent a product that will make it possible."

"Good luck," said Dummy.

Smarty called a bank and requested a meeting with a business banker and an insurance banker and a few other bankers. At the meeting, Smarty told the bankers what his plans were. They all looked at the old typewriter, thinking, *That is impossible*. One of the bankers said, "No way. No one can create something better than a typewriter, not to mention sending a note or letter that would only take seconds for the recipient to receive it." All the bankers looked at each other and said, "This is impossible. How can you do that? Oh really, I would like to see it with my own eyes to believe this." All inventors hear these words.

Then Smarty asked the bankers, "Did you ever want to become a rich man when you were younger?"

No one said anything because it is hard to make a million dollars.

Smarty said, "Men, see you" and walked out.

When Smarty got home his mother asked him how the meeting with the business bankers went, and Smarty replied, "Mom, their attitude was poor; they all wanted to be poor. This type of mental attitude will not give us a positive result."

Chapter II
THE SECOND MEETING:

It was a Friday when Smarty told his brother Dummy that he was meeting some other business banker at a nearby bank. The older brother said, "Do you want to stay here and play video games with me?" Smarty said, "No, brother, I do not have time to play around."

Smarty went to the bank and this time he met a business banker who was very smart. He asked Smarty, "Do you have a business plan?" Smarty said yes and the banker read the plan and said, "That is terrific. I love this. I can I help you."

Smarty said, "Are you a rich man?"

The banker said, "No, I am not rich."

Then Smarty asked him, "When you were younger did you want to be rich?"

The business banker said, "Yes, of course, and I am looking forward to making my million."

Smarty said, "My man, I think you might be the right guy. I am raising capital for my business and I need financing."

"I will put a team of business advisors together to work with you, and I will direct you to a business trainer and a grant writer. I will connect you with the right business development center. I will prepare an SBA business loan for you. I will connect you with a product insurance banker. We will work together to get this done."

Smarty heard the word "we" and realized this banker was smart; he had ambition, he was motivated, and he was a doer. Smarty said to the banker, "I like your spirit and attitude."

The banker answered, "I love technology and I know this will create a lot of opportunity."

Five years later Smarty introduced the Internet. We have Facebook, Google, and so on. Because of one invention all these other services were born. Now let us not forget the banker who always wanted to be rich. Smarty asked him to invest in his company and now the banker has millions in his bank account.

Dummy asked his brother Smarty, "How did the banker become so rich?"

Smarty said, "His mental attitude made him a rich man. When I walked in the bank showing him my plan, he quickly saw opportunity for himself. He used his brain, making all the contacts and putting a team in place. That is all he had to do."

Chapter 12
OUR MINDS

Smarty and Dummy, when they were young men, lived in separate bedrooms. One Saturday, Dummy entered Smarty's bedroom and noticed that it was neat and organized and asked his younger brother, "Why is your bedroom always clean and neat?"

"Well, brother, do you love gardens, plants, and flowers?"

"Yes," answered Dummy.

"Can I enter your bedroom to see how you organize it?"

"Sure, brother."

When Smarty went inside the bedroom, he noticed Dummy's book bag was on the floor and his books were on the floor and the bedroom smelled like smoke. "Do you smoke, brother?"

"Yes, I do smoke."

"Well, brother, smoking is not good for your mind." Smarty asked Dummy to step outside and take a look at the garden. "What do you notice?"

"Well, brother, this garden is neat."

"Do you see any wild grass, Dummy? Just like a garden, you must treat your mind right. The reason your room is so messy is because your mind is full of grass; if you stop smoking and eat food like baked fish and vegetables, these foods are good for your mind."

"Thank you, brother, I will try very hard to stop smoking."

For a full year Dummy stopped smoking. He noticed a great improvement in his habits: his room remained clean, he started setting goals, he planned his daily, weekly, and monthly activities, and Dummy started seeing a great change for the better in his personal life.

Smarty said to his brother, "Just like I take good care of the garden—the flowers, I fertilize them every other day—you should treat your mind the same, because the mind is a beautiful, precious, and powerful organ. Everything that you are enjoying today is the fruit and the product of our mind. The bicycle, airplane, car, boat, train, cell phone—all are the direct result of someone who put in some serious thought to innovate these great products. Yes, we owe our mind a great deal of gratitude. Think of something we did not have four years ago. Today you may be using something new; this is because someone was busy thinking of something useful. It takes a great deal of imagination to come up with a new product."

Chapter 13
THE HOUSECLEANER AND HER ATTITUDE:

Smarty became very rich, and he proclaimed himself king. His mother loved him very much. When Smarty turned thirty years old his mother said, "Son, it is time to find yourself a wife."

Smarty replied, "It is hard to find the right woman. If it is time to find myself a wife, I need her to be just like you."

"What do you mean by that?" his mother asked.

"Well, Mother, I cannot find a woman who cooks like you or who is as clean as you, Mother. You keep this castle very clean. I have an idea! What if we hire a maid who you like, and you can teach her your ways of preparing my food, show her the way I like things, teach her how to keep this castle neat. Explain to her how picky I am, tell her about my good habits and bad habits, tell her everything she needs to know about me."

"Very well," said his mother, "that sounds good to me." Therefore, she hired a housecleaner who someday the king would ask to marry him.

The mother hired a maid, a beautiful girl named Olivia, just like the king asked, without thinking, and she taught her everything about the king. She taught her how to cook Smarty's favorite food and most importantly the mother said the king loved to see his castle remain neat and clean. Therefore, Olivia would carry out her duty each day.

One Saturday, the king and his mother went out and purchased an engagement ring which cost a million dollars. Before they departed for the castle, the king, who planned to have a huge party that night, invited all the girls in town. At midnight the king would choose a girl among all the girls who were invited, however, never reveal to Olivia she would be the chosen one.

That day Smarty's mother told Olivia, "Today is the last day you will clean the castle," and asked her to prepare Smarty's favorite food. "Make sure to prepare all his favorite songs."

Olivia said to herself, "Well, since today is the last day I will clean this castle and prepare his food, I will not prepare Smarty's favorite food." She left the entrance of the palace dirty;

she did not prepare the king's favorite songs; she demonstrated total dislike for the king and was not polite to him.

The king felt so sad the night he was supposed to ask her to marry him. Smarty said to his mother, "She does not love me. Cancel the ceremony."

His mother said, "Do not worry, son, I will find you another girl. Olivia was not the right girl."

She found another maid, whose name was Josephine. The king's mother taught her everything about her son, how to prepare his favorite food and his favorite music and so on.

One Sunday, the mother told Josephine, "There is going to be a party. Clean the castle, make sure everything is neat, and prepare his favorite food and songs. There is going to be an engagement party."

Josephine did everything right for the king and never complained. Josephine's friends asked her not to come to the party. "This party does not concern you," they said.

The king noticed that Josephine did not get dressed up for the engagement party and he sent an employee to ask Josephine to attend. He wanted to introduce Josephine to everyone and tell everyone that the delicious food was prepared by Josephine.

At midnight the king was supposed to choose his future wife. When midnight came, all the girls lined up and the king asked one girl this question: "Would you accept this rose and have a dance with the choosing one?" After the midnight bell stopped ringing, the ballroom was so quiet, and the king noticed that Josephine was not in line. She did not think the king would ever choose her.

The king stood up and said, "Where is Josephine? I don't see her." Everyone was calling for her; she was all the way in the back. The king said, "Josephine, would you come forward?"

She said, "Yes, my king."

The king said, "Josephine, when I invited you to come work in this castle, you did your job and never complained or asked for anything more. Most of all, your attitude impresses me. Everyone who came to work here, the only thing that concerned them was more money. You help Mother keep this castle neat and clean, and you prepare my food just like my mother. I love you, Josephine. Would you accept this rose?"

"Yes," Josephine replied.

"Would you accept this ring?"

"Yes."

"Would you marry me?"

"Yes," she replied.

Four years later they were married and had four children together. Twelve years later the mother of the king said to Josephine, "I am glad I met you and had the opportunity to teach you everything about my son," and she died happily at the age of ninety-six.

Chapter 14
ATTITUDE

Smarty owned a car manufacturing plant and had many employees. There was one particular employee who was very reliable, motivated, and took his work seriously. Dummy helped assemble millions of cars. Those days there were not too many robots in manufacturing facilities to help the employees with their chores. This employee would work very hard. People who bought cars from this manufacturer would compliment this car company for making such a reliable car. Dummy worked there for twenty-five years and then decided to retire. When Smarty heard that, he thought, *Besides money and a party, what can we offer him as a token of appreciation? Well, maybe a nice vacation.*

"Well," Smarty said, "we will ask him to assemble one last car." So the month he was supposed to retire, Smarty called Dummy and said, "We know you helped us build many cars. Can you do us a favor?"

"Yes, what is it? What do you want me to help you with?"

Smarty said, "We want you to build one last car. Is that okay with you?"

"Sure!"

"Take your time and assemble a very nice car; put the best stuff in this car and the most expensive material."

Dummy said, "Who is the car for? Who is buying it is?"

Smarty answered, "Well, we will donate this car to charity for our church."

Dummy said to himself, "Since this is the last car I will assemble, who cares about a car for church." He ordered cheap parts, and assembled poor-quality materials. He built the car so fast and within a week the car was put together. Dummy called Smarty and said, "Well, the car is ready."

Smarty said, "Do me one more favor."

Dummy said, "What is it you want me to do?"

"Test drive the car to your house and tell me how it drives."

"Sure." On his way home Dummy said, "I did a poor job on this car. I did not put in a

GPS system, Bluetooth, or CD player. I did not even put air-conditioning and keyless entry in this car." When he got home he called Smarty and said the car drove well.

Smarty said, "Remember I told you to take your time and put the best materials in this car. Well, as a token of appreciation, the last car we asked you to build is yours. We give it to you as a gift for all your hard work. Keep it as a souvenir."

Dummy had the chance to build a 400,000-dollar car, and he did not. He said to himself, "Now I remember what my grandma told me. She said your attitude can take you to heaven or it can take you to hell."

Chapter 15
THE MOTHER GOAT OK

A female goat said, "Someday I will have four baby goats. When I find the right husband, we will live in a big house with a lot of trees and a vegetable farm full of spinach, lettuce, kale, beets, sweet yams, and a river not too far from my farm. There I will teach my goats how to swim, and a school nearby. Most importantly, I will be good to all my baby goats."

Not too long afterward, the goat was mature enough to be married. In those days when goats turned twelve years of age they were allowed to be married providing that they received the blessing from their elders. When the goat met Mr. Dammy, they fell in love, got engaged, and planned their wedding. Soon after they found a farm by the river and a house. They were very happy. Mother Goat had four baby goats; however, things did not turn out the way she wanted.

One of the baby goats was different. Everything he touched turned to silver and his name was Make. When he was in school, he was admired and loved by all his teachers. One day the principal sent a gold letter to his mother indicating how smart Make was; his writing teacher was also impressed with him because he was a creative writer. Not only that, Make had a magic hand; he could create things that were useful. The neighbors also were so pleased with Make because he was nice, kind, loveable, and helpful. Most people in the neighborhood loved him. His sisters and brothers were not too happy that everyone was saying nice things about him, and this caused jealousy among them. What is a mother to do in this situation?

A Mother's Attitude:

Mother Goat was also jealous of her son for being so talented, and she decided not to feed him. In the morning they did not give him a ride to school, not even money for transportation; they were oppressing him financially. After school students had money to purchase lunch, but not Make. Often he would go a whole day in school without food. He had grown accustomed to that. This type of attitude did not have an impact on him; he continued to be motivated and be nice to everyone in the family.

One day the goats' parents went on vacation and left them in the house for a month. Make's brother hid food from him and decided to starve him. After three weeks Make became sick from starvation and could not get up from his bed because he was ill enough to die.

Meanwhile three thieves were passing by and noticed Alee, who was 200 pounds; Ball, who was 220 pounds; and Celine, who was 250 pounds. The thieves wondered, "What have these goats been eating? They are as big as cows." The thieves did not want Make because he was so weak and was about twenty pounds. The thieves did not like Make because he had no meat on his body. The thieves decided to take Alee, Ball, and Celine.

When the parents returned from vacation, they entered the house and noticed all the goats were gone. As for Make, he was so sick, and explained to his parents he was starved by his brother and sisters, and thieves had come by and taken his brothers and sisters.

Mother Goat was so sad. Now she only had one goat to care for.

Chapter 16
THE LOSER LEFT HIS WIFE

Smarty and Dummy were married to lovely wives. Dummy had two children, a boy and a girl. For twelve years Dummy had a very wonderful family. They did things all great families do: go on vacation, go to parties, Broadway shows, and concerts, and every Friday they would gather and have family dinner.

Dummy's wife was a stay-at-home mom who took care of the family. She made sure all the kids' homework was done, took them to the library, and participated in all her children's activities, and for Dummy, this was a perfect life. Every day after work he would find fresh food; something fresh and different would be at the dinner table for him to eat. Meanwhile, when all the kids went to bed at 8 p.m., Hillary, Dummy's wife, took classes. Someday her children would be twelve to sixteen and they would not need much help from their mother. She planned to find a job then; however, Dummy loved the fact that his wife was always home. He had a job making fifteen cents every two weeks. The year was 1896 and life was perfect until his wife said, "Hubby, the kids are all mature now. I need to find a job." Dummy was not too pleased with that. A few years later Dummy's wife started earning more money than he did. Dummy was unhappy and noticed that his wife was buying the kids more toys and goodies, and that made him more unhappy and he left his wife for someone else. He remarried and the second wife also after a few years started making more money than he did. Now he wondered, "Maybe I should not have left my first wife," and he decided to leave the second wife. He went back to his hometown to ask his first wife to get back with him again. "You divorced me and our children because I made more money than you; now your second wife makes more money than you," the first wife said. "I am sorry but you are a loser. You don't know what you want in life."

Now the first wife is engaged to be married sometime this year, to a man who knows what he wants in life.

Chapter 17
COURTESY

Three brothers, Smarty, the Bad, and Dummy, attended the same school and went home at the same time after school. One day Smarty saw a blind woman crossing the street and heading in the wrong direction. Smarty said, "Excuse me, ma'am, you are heading toward the red light. May I help you?"

"Certainly," replied the old woman.

The bad brother said, "Are you out of your mind? That old woman looks crazy and she looks dirty; you should not have helped her."

Dummy said, "That is true. Why are you wasting your time helping people? You have to worry about yourself."

When they arrived in front of their building, there was a young lady with groceries trying to get in, but having a hard time opening the building door. Smarty once again held the door for this young lady and helped her carry her groceries up to her apartment. The lady said, "That is very kind of you. I'd just like you to know I have a bad shoulder, and it was a blessing when you offered to carry my groceries upstairs." She asked Smarty for his name and said, "It is a pleasure meeting you."

The Bad and Dummy said, "Not us. It was not a pleasure to meet you. Now you have made us late for our basketball game."

The next day, the three brothers were on the train and the lady Smarty had helped carry her groceries got on the train; however, there were no seats available. Smarty offered the lady his seat, and she said, "Thank you. That is the second time you helped me. I had a long day at work. You are a blessing, Smarty, and thank you for giving me your seat."

The Bad and Dummy said, "Well, woman, you are lucky because if it were us, we would have never offered our seat to you."

The woman was about to get off the train and said, "Thank you, Smarty, you are so kind; your mother did a good job on you."

During a summer vacation, the three brothers needed a summer job, so they went to Manhattan for a job interview. The lady on the train was the interviewer. She was so happy to meet Smarty one more time, and this time the lady was the one to help Smarty get the job.

Chapter 18
THE PROCRASTINATOR

Smarty and Dummy are very different. Smarty gets things done very fast and plans his days, weeks, months, and years. He leaves nothing for later or tomorrow, yet he is a very busy man. When you ask Smarty to do something, you can count on him; however, his brother Dummy has all the excuses in the book as to why he is so busy, or he will say, "I'll do it next week."

Smarty tells him to save some money for retirement but Dummy says, "I have time. I am young. I have enough time to save at the age of twenty." He is supposed to open a 401(k) or invest in the stock market but he says, "I am young. I will do it when I am thirty years old." When he turns thirty, he says, "I am young. Now is the time to have fun. I don't want to worry about that yet. Don't rush me. I have a good seventy years to enjoy my life."

Life goes by and Dummy is always saying he has time to get things done, and when he was in school he often waited until the last minute to do his homework and study; however, he is a generous man who loves to help people and share whatever he has. For Thanksgiving he buys turkey and feeds the homeless. He is good at heart.

He is now eighty years old and he never did get anything done, no money for retirement, no life insurance, no real state investment. He lives from day to day, not worrying about the future. He one day dies and before doing all the things he thought he had time to do. On his way to heaven, he meets the guardian angels who will show him what he did when he was on earth. Everything he did well is written in a big book. The condition for entering heaven is you have to do many good deeds while you were on earth and you cannot commit suicide; if you do, you will not enter heaven.

After the angels finish reading the book of good deeds, they find that Dummy did many good things and was very generous and caring, loveable and kind. The angels say to Dummy, "You have a choice. You can enter heaven or you can go back to earth. When people die, most would rather enter heaven, and here is why.

"First, at a distance they are able to see their mother, grandma, grandpa, husband, wife, and if they had a daughter or son who had died before them. Imagine you have not seen your loved one for thirty years; that is why when a person dies they choose heaven rather than earth."

Dummy replies, "I will go back to earth to do all the things I thought I had time to do."

Therefore, the angels return Dummy to earth for being kind and generous. On earth Dummy starts setting daily goals; first he buys life insurance, he starts putting some money in the bank, and he writes a book he always wanted to write. When people ask Dummy, "Why are you setting goals for everything you have to do?" Dummy says, "Being a procrastinator is not a good thing."

The writing part is for ages six and up.

What have you learned from the story?

_____

_____

_____

_____

_____

_____

_____

_____

_____

_____

_____

_____

_____

_____

_____

_____

_____

_____

_____

_____

The writing part is for ages six and up.

What have you learned from the story on page 1?

_____

_____

_____

_____

_____

_____

_____

_____

_____

_____

_____

_____

_____

_____

_____

_____

_____

_____

_____

_____

The reading part is for ages six and up.

What have you learned from the story on page 2?

_____

_____

_____

_____

_____

_____

_____

_____

_____

_____

_____

_____

_____

_____

_____

_____

_____

_____

_____

_____

The reading part is for ages six and up.

What have you learned from the story on page 3?

_____

_____

_____

_____

_____

_____

_____

_____

_____

_____

_____

_____

_____

_____

_____

_____

_____

_____

_____

_____

_____

The reading part is for ages six and up.

What have you learned from the story on page 4?

_____

_____

_____

_____

_____

_____

_____

_____

_____

_____

_____

_____

_____

_____

_____

_____

_____

_____

_____

_____

_____

_____

_____

The writing part is for ages six and up.

What have you learned from the story on page 5?

_____

_____

_____

_____

_____

_____

_____

_____

_____

_____

_____

_____

_____

_____

_____

_____

_____

_____

_____

_____

The writing part is for ages six and up.

What have you learned from the story on page 6?

_____

_____

_____

_____

_____

_____

_____

_____

_____

_____

_____

_____

_____

_____

_____

_____

_____

_____

_____

_____

_____

_____

_____

The writing part is for ages six and up.

What have you learned from the story on page 7?

_____

_____

_____

_____

_____

_____

_____

_____

_____

_____

_____

_____

_____

_____

_____

_____

_____

_____

_____

The writing part is for ages six and up.

What have you learned from the story on page 8?

_____

_____

_____

_____

_____

_____

_____

_____

_____

_____

_____

_____

_____

_____

_____

_____

_____

_____

_____

_____

_____

The writing part is for ages six and up.

What have you learned from the story on page 9?

_____

_____

_____

_____

_____

_____

_____

_____

_____

_____

_____

_____

_____

_____

_____

_____

_____

_____

_____

_____

_____

_____

_____

The writing part is for ages six and up.

What have you learned from the story on page 10?

_____

_____

_____

_____

_____

_____

_____

_____

_____

_____

_____

_____

_____

_____

_____

_____

_____

_____

_____

_____

_____

The writing part is for ages six and up.

What have you learned from the story on page 11?

_____

_____

_____

_____

_____

_____

_____

_____

_____

_____

_____

_____

_____

_____

_____

_____

_____

_____

_____

_____

The writing part is for ages six and up.

What have you learned from the story on page 12?

_____

_____

_____

_____

_____

_____

_____

_____

_____

_____

_____

_____

_____

_____

_____

_____

_____

_____

_____

_____

The writing part is for ages six and up.

What have you learned from the story on page 13?

_____

_____

_____

_____

_____

_____

_____

_____

_____

_____

_____

_____

_____

_____

_____

_____

_____

_____

_____

The writing part is for ages six and up.

What have you learned from the story on page 14?

_____

_____

_____

_____

_____

_____

_____

_____

_____

_____

_____

_____

_____

_____

_____

_____

_____

_____

_____

_____

_____

The writing part is for ages six and up.

What have you learned from the story on page 15?

_____

_____

_____

_____

_____

_____

_____

_____

_____

_____

_____

_____

_____

_____

_____

_____

_____

_____

_____

_____

_____

The writing part is for ages six and up.

What have you learned from the story on page 16?

_____

_____

_____

_____

_____

_____

_____

_____

_____

_____

_____

_____

_____

_____

_____

_____

_____

_____

_____

_____

_____

The writing part is for ages six and up.

What have you learned from the story on page 17?

_____

_____

_____

_____

_____

_____

_____

_____

_____

_____

_____

_____

_____

_____

_____

_____

_____

_____

_____

_____

_____

The writing part is for ages six and up.

What have you learned from the story on page 18?

_____

_____

_____

_____

_____

_____

_____

_____

_____

_____

_____

_____

_____

_____

_____

_____

_____

_____

_____

The writing part is for ages six and up.

Do you know someone who is like Smarty? Write what you like about this person.

_____

_____

_____

_____

_____

_____

_____

_____

_____

_____

_____

_____

_____

_____

_____

_____

_____

_____

_____

_____

The writing part is for ages six and up.

Do you know a person who is like Dummy? Write what you like or do not like about this person.

_____

_____

_____

_____

_____

_____

_____

_____

_____

_____

_____

_____

_____

_____

_____

_____

_____

_____

The writing part is for ages six and up.

Do you know someone like Smarty, The Bad, and Dummy? Write what you have learned from these three characters.

_____

_____

_____

_____

_____

_____

_____

_____

_____

_____

_____

_____

_____

_____

_____

_____

_____

_____

_____

The writing part is for ages six and up.

Write a story about your mother. For example, where did your mother meet your dad?

_____

_____

_____

_____

_____

_____

_____

_____

_____

_____

_____

_____

_____

_____

_____

_____

_____

_____

_____

_____

_____

The writing part is for ages six and up.

Write a story about your dad; explain why it is important for you to write about him.

_____

_____

_____

_____

_____

_____

_____

_____

_____

_____

_____

_____

_____

_____

_____

_____

_____

_____

_____

_____

_____

Write a story about your school. What do you like or do not like about your school?

How do you plan to help make your school better? Write what your intentions are in making your school better. Is there anyone you like or dislike in your school? Write what your intentions and your plans are in helping resolve your issues.

Make certain your teachers or your school advisor read this essay.

_____

_____

_____

_____

_____

_____

_____

_____

_____

_____

_____

_____

_____

_____

_____

_____

_____

_____

_____

_____

The writing part is for ages six and up.

Do you have any goals for the week, month, this year or next year?

Write down your goals here.

_____

_____

_____

_____

_____

_____

_____

_____

_____

_____

_____

_____

_____

_____

_____

_____

_____

_____

READING METHOD PART 2
IS COMING SOON.

These instructions are only for your four- and five-year-old:

I am certain if these instructions are followed, 96 percent of four- and five-year-old will start reading within a week to one month. If you notice your child does not develop the aptitude for reading, do not blame anyone. Some parents blame teachers, but should not. You as a parent must take a proactive **attitude** toward your child's academic success.

Here are the instructions to activate the reading **genius** inside the mind of your child; this is very **important**. Once the genius is activated, there is no going back. The aptitude toward reading will **start shining.** Your child's mind will never be the same once you start this approach.

First, you need a room with no distractions, which includes no **music** or **television.**

Hide and seek **find** the word:

Fist show your students or child the word, which is visual, your students or child need to see the word very important visual acknowledge the word.

Say the word hearing very important.

Have the students **repeat** the word verbally very important.

Ask your students or child **write the word down on a decoding work book** see Amazon. com or Outskirtspress for a decoding work book.

Most importantly do not start reading the paragraph in the main story. What you must do is, the words that are arrange VERTICALLY that is where you will start showing by pointing finger at the word, saying the word and ask your students or child to reap the word verbally then ask your student to find the word.

For example the word mama, after your students or child see it say it and write it, right the way now go in the first paragraph first line by pointing your finger in the first paraph and the first line ask your students or child to find the word mama.

Repeat this process for each word you in the vertical row. Now when the find all the words in the paragraph. You can begin reading the paragraph by allowing your child to see the word and say the word after you. You may want to read the paragraph two times, Then ask your students or child to read the paragraph.

Start with the vertical word first and do each word at a time, what will be the result for some students, they will start reading right the way for others it might take a few days. Individual result may vary each child is different.

Acknowledge the key word that make this method a miracle see page 78.

Knowing how to read is important , However, **understand** what you read is <u>more important</u>.

I would suggest these two books which I believe are a most.

Decoding the reading obstacle increase your test scores in English and Science.

Work book for top producer.
See amazon.com or Outskirts Press
Walker Guerrier

Page 78.
The key word is **FIND**
This word **FIND** bring out all the excitement, focus and attention use this method in your class room ask the students who can find the word Mama see the result for yourself.

READING METHOD PART 2
TO BE CONTINUED

www.ingramcontent.com/pod-product-compliance
Lightning Source LLC
Chambersburg PA
CBHW081604170526
45166CB00009B/2822